DISCARDED

SECRET

⭐ ## OF THE

SUFFOCATING

SLIME TRAP ⭐

... AND MORE!

BY ANA MARÍA RODRÍGUEZ

Enslow Publishers, Inc.
40 Industrial Road
Box 398
Berkeley Heights, NJ 07922
USA

http://www.enslow.com

Acknowledgments

The author would like to express her immense gratitude to all the scientists who have contributed to the *Animal Secrets Revealed!* series. Their comments and photos have been invaluable to the creation of these books.

Library of Congress Cataloging-in-Publication Data

Rodriguez, Ana Maria, 1958–
  Secret of the suffocating slime trap— and more! / Ana María Rodríguez.
    p. cm. — (Animal secrets revealed!)
  Summary: "Explains how hagfish excrete slime to evade predators and details other strange abilities of different types of animals"—Provided by publisher.
  Includes bibliographical references and index.
  ISBN-13: 978-0-7660-2954-5
  ISBN-10: 0-7660-2954-9
  1. Fishes—Juvenile literature. 2. Fishes—Research—Juvenile literature. I. Title.
QL617.2.R65 2009
597—dc22
                    2007039493

Printed in the United States of America

10 9 8 7 6 5 4 3 2 1

To Our Readers: We have done our best to make sure all Internet Addresses in this book were active and appropriate when we went to press. However, the author and the publisher have no control over and assume no liability for the material available on those Internet sites or on other Web sites they may link to. Any comments or suggestions can be sent by e-mail to comments@enslow.com or to the address on the back cover.

♻ Enslow Publishers, Inc., is committed to printing our books on recycled paper. The paper in every book contains 10% to 30% post-consumer waste (PCW). The cover board on the outside of each book contains 100% PCW. Our goal is to do our part to help young people and the environment too!

Illustration Credits: Alcatel-Lucent Bell Labs, pp. 37, 40, 42; C. Ortlepp, p. 7; Dr. Garth Fletcher, Memorial University of Newfoundland, Canada, pp. 14, 17, 19; Esta Spalding, p. 12; J.D. Crawford, L.B. Fletcher and E. Stipetic, reproduced from J Exp Biol. 204(2): 175–183, 2001 with permission of the authors and the Company of Biologists, p. 27; Kim Taylor/Minden Pictures, p. 31; Sara Östlund-Nilsson, University of Oslo, pp. 32, 33; Simon Quellen Field <http://scitoys.com>, p. 24; with permission of Dr. Jeanette Lim and the Company of Biologists, pp. 9, 11.

Cover Illustration: Esta Spalding

★ CONTENTS ★

★

ENTER THE WORLD OF ANIMAL SECRETS!

In this volume of *Animal Secrets Revealed!* four different types of sea creatures will surprise you. The apparently simple hagfish can be very quick to release a sticky and slimy trap that would mean big trouble for any predator. The flat, one-sided flounder will show you how it fights freezing from the inside out.

The elephantnose fish may not be able to see much in its muddy, African environment, but ear stones and bubbles make this fish a good listener. The little, colorful, three-spined stickleback has an unexpected side: it gets hooked on decorating! Finally, the intriguing and shy brittle star does not have eyes or a brain but it sure knows how to "keep an eye" on everything! Welcome to the world of animal secrets!

1
SLICK AND SLIME

The severed head of a dead fish with its mouth propped open looked a little odd, it is true. This unusual setting for a science experiment provoked strange looks from people who wandered into the lab. Jeanette Lim, Douglas Fudge, and John Gosline noticed the looks but kept doing the experiment. It was no joke. They were seriously studying how hagfish slime works.[1]

Slime Attack!

The eel-shaped body of a hagfish rests on the bottom of a fish tank. The fish has no eyes, no jaws, no teeth, and no fins—it must be easy to grab. Not quite. Before you can say "Gotcha!" the hagfish squirts ooze into the surrounding seawater. The ooze comes out through numerous holes lined up along its slender body. In an instant, the ooze swells several hundred times its initial volume and traps your hand in a gooey, sticky mass. Yuck! You have been the victim of an amazing defense strategy.

Douglas Fudge and his colleagues are intrigued by how hagfish can turn perfectly liquid water into a viscous, sticky slime in a fraction of a second. The slime is not like your ordinary slimy goo, like the one made by snails. "When you lift hagfish slime into the air, most of the water runs out of the slime," explains Fudge.[2] What gives this slime its intriguing properties? Fudge decided to find out.

Of Slippery Mucus and Ultra-Thin Strings

Fudge and his colleagues observed that hagfish slime is made mostly of seawater. The hagfish provided less than one hundredth of one percent of the

slime's weight. Nevertheless, when the hagfish squirts its ooze into seawater, the mixture expands tremendously, trapping lots of water in its structure.

Hagfish are the only fish to tie themselves in a knot. They do it to squeeze their own slime from their bodies.

Hagfish slime is made of three components. One is seawater and the other two are produced by the hagfish. One is mucins (or mucus), which are proteins linked to carbohydrates. They give the slime its slippery feel. The other component is fibers that are as thin as spider silk. They are about two micrometers in diameter and twelve centimeters long (about five inches). These fibers make hagfish slime different from other slimes, like snail slime—which does not have fibers.[3]

These ultra-thin fibers are very strong and flexible. When fibers and mucins get together in seawater, they form a structure that behaves like a fine sieve or strainer. The sieve is capable of trapping water loosely in a viscous, sticky

KNOTTING AWAY THE SLIME TRAP

Sometimes, hagfish get caught in their own mass of slime. But unlike other fish, hagfish have a neat trick to find freedom. The hagfish contorts itself into a tight overhand knot and then passes the knot down along its whole body. As the knot slides, it wipes the slime off the fish's skin. Hagfish are the only animals known to tie themselves in a knot![4]

environment. This has an appearance similar to gelatin that is beginning to set.[5]

Fudge and his colleagues suspected that if a hagfish predator got caught in a slime trap, it would be in serious trouble. What if the predator was another fish that breathes through gills? What if those gills became entangled with the sticky, gooey slime? Lim, Fudge, and Gosline needed the head of a dead fish to test the effect of the hagfish slime on real gills. Lim went shopping at her local supermarket.

Dead Fish Head Setup

Lim returned from the supermarket carrying heads of China rockfish. To test the effect of hagfish slime on the gills, the scientists tightly fitted a fish head inside a PVC pipe. PVC pipes are white, hard plastic pipes like those that carry water inside houses.

They pushed the fish head through one of the pipe's ends to a point just behind the eyes and in front of the gills. They secured the fish head inside the pipe. The scientists used a wire oval ring to keep the fish's mouth open. They wanted the water to flow freely inside the mouth and through the gills, like in a live fish. They placed the whole fish head setup inside a twenty-liter aquarium containing artificial seawater.[6]

The scientists measured how much water flowed through the gills in the presence and in the absence of slime. If the water flow slowed down in the presence of slime, then this would be bad news for a live fish caught in a slime trap.

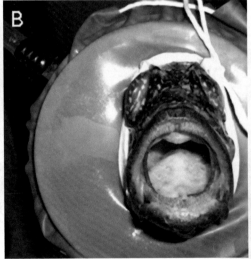

Side (A) and front (B) views of the apparatus for measuring the effect of hagfish slime on water flow through fish gills.

In nature, this jawless fish eats mostly carrion or dead animals it finds in the sea. It usually digs into the dead body, eating the insides first. Although in the distant past the jawless fish were once a diverse group on Earth, the seventy species of hagfish and thirty-four species of lampreys are the only representatives of this group that exist today.[7]

Slower water flow means that the fish might not get enough oxygen delivered into its body through the gills. The fish might die from the suffocating slime. Is hagfish slime that dangerous to gill-breathing fish?

Hagfish in Action

The scientists had the fish head ready inside the aquarium and the water flowing through the fish's mouth. They gently placed a live hagfish in the aquarium and waited a few seconds to let the fish get used to the place. They turned on a high-speed video camera. They began measuring the water flow through the dead fish gills.

Now it was time for the hagfish to do its sliming trick. One of the scientists pinched a small area of the hagfish's tail with padded pincers. Immediately, the gland in the hole in the pinched area powerfully squirted out a jet of ooze. At the same time, the hagfish vigorously thrashed about the aquarium, clearly responding to the pinch. The thrashing movement helped the ooze mix with the water and expand fully into a gooey mass.[8]

The scientists recorded the water flow through the dead fish gills. The results showed them how dangerous a gooey trap might be.

A Sticky Dangerous Trap

The researchers analyzed the results of changes in water flow through the gills and watched the videos they had taken

Hagfish slime was hard to remove from the gills after it got trapped inside the rockfish's mouth.

Gemma Fudge, Dr. Fudge's daughter, enjoys getting her hands on hagfish slime, while her friend Emilie Jorgensen observes.

during the experiments. They observed that as soon as the slimy water began entering the dead fish's mouth, the flow through the gills decreased up to eight times the rate before the slime attack.[9]

When the scientists looked at the dead fish head after the experiment they saw that most of the slime was trapped inside the mouth. Sometimes, it even stuck out of the mouth. A tangle of mucus and slime threads coated the gills. If this were a live fish, it would quickly die.

Lim, Fudge, and Gosline had proved that the intriguing hagfish slime can be a deadly trap for predators.

2
FISH FIGHT THE BIG FREEZE

It was really bad news for Choy Hew. It got very cold that winter night in Newfoundland. All his codfish in the outdoor seawater tank had frozen to death. Hew was counting on having those fish alive for his research on insulin (a hormone that helps regulate blood sugar). Now all he had was plenty of cod for dinner!

Hew went to see the seawater tank. Yes, all the cod were dead, but there was also a surprise in the tank. Some fish, called winter flounder, were swimming on the bottom of the same tank. They were totally unaffected by the icy temperature. The obvious question formed in Hew's mind, "How come these flat fish did not freeze to death?"[1]

> **Science Tongue Twister:**
> *The winter flounder's scientific name is* **Pseudopleuronectes americanus.**

Fighting Freezing from the Inside Out

Garth Fletcher, Hew's colleague, suggested that the winter flounder in the tank might have been protected by antifreeze proteins in their blood, like some Antarctic fish. These proteins prevent freezing of the organism that carries them. They do so by stopping ice crystals from growing into large, deadly frozen masses.

Hew was hooked. From then on, he forgot about the insulin project with cod and studied antifreeze proteins in flounder. By the late 1980s, Hew and other scientists had discovered and extensively studied an antifreeze protein in winter

Winter flounder rest at the bottom of the water tank at the Ocean Sciences Centre, Memorial University of Newfoundland, Canada, where they do not freeze.

flounder called "type I." However, this turned out to be just part of the antifreeze secret of this fascinating fish.[2]

The Mystery Molecule

Scientists thought that type I antifreeze proteins were the clue to the winter flounder's survival in freezing seawater. But when they studied the proteins in detail they found puzzling results.

Scientists learned from lab experiments that flounder blood without any antifreeze proteins would freeze at -0.8 degrees Celsius (30.6 degrees Fahrenheit). If type I antifreeze proteins were present in the blood, it would freeze at a lower temperature, -1.5°C (29.3°F). If the temperature dropped below -1.5°C, however, type I proteins could not stop ice from forming. This is the puzzle: When the outdoor tank froze, scientists realized that winter flounder can survive when seawater freezes, which is at -1.9°C (28.6°F). But if type I antifreeze proteins only protected down to -1.5°C, what was protecting flounders from freezing when the temperature dropped to -1.9°C?[3]

It was clear to scientists that there had to be something else in flounder blood that prevented the fish from becoming a frozen meal.

Meet the Scientists: *Christopher Marshall, Garth Fletcher, and Peter Davies are biologists and biochemists at Queen's University in Ontario and Memorial University of Newfoundland, Canada. They study how animals manage to survive in extreme environments.*

The Colder, the Better

As other scientists had done before, Christopher Marshall and his colleagues did not test the antifreeze activity in whole blood. They tested it in plasma, the liquid part of blood that is left after white and red blood cells are removed. But unlike other scientists before them, Marshall and his colleagues tested the antifreeze activity in flounder plasma that had never warmed up to room temperature. Previously, the plasma had been collected, frozen, and thawed to do the experiments. Marshall's sample had always stayed cold.[4]

When they tested this plasma, they found that it did not freeze until the temperature was well below -2°C (28.4°F). This was more than enough to protect the fish at the freezing point of seawater (-1.9°C, 28.6°F). The never-warmed plasma contained the mystery molecule that was responsible for the flounder staying unfrozen.

Lemons and Double Pyramids

To take a closer look at the mystery molecule, Marshall and his colleagues used a microscope to study the shape of the microcrystals formed by the molecule to prevent freezing. The scientists knew that different antifreeze molecules create ice crystals in different three-dimensional shapes. Type I antifreeze molecules, for example, shape the crystals like double-hexagonal micro-pyramids.[5] What shape would the crystals in the plasma be?

Cheryl Barron, a student at Memorial University of Newfoundland, is using a microscope to measure antifreeze activity in fish blood. The computer monitor shows a magnified view of the crystals growing under the microscope.

Using a microscope connected to a computer monitor, the scientists saw the shapes of the ice crystals formed in flounder plasma. The ice crystals were not double-hexagonal pyramids like those formed by type I antifreeze; they were oval like a lemon. This proved the presence of the unknown mystery molecule.[6]

Plasma Popsicles Anyone?

Marshall and his colleagues had found out that the antifreeze mystery molecule needed to stay cold to form tiny lemon-shaped crystals. So, the scientists did all the experiments in a walk-in refrigerator.

To separate the mystery molecule from the many other molecules in plasma, Marshall grew an ice popsicle in diluted, or watered-down, plasma. The trick was to grow the ice in the popsicle very slowly. In this way, as the popsicle grew, only antifreeze molecules, which specifically bind to the crystals, would be included in the ice. After the popsicle had formed some sixteen hours later, Marshall thawed the popsicle and collected the purified mystery antifreeze molecule.[7]

Not Just Active, Hyperactive

The mystery molecules and type I antifreeze proteins both bind to ice. However, the former protect against freezing at a

SAME JOB, DIFFERENT SHAPES

Antifreeze proteins have also been found in other types of fish, insects, plants, and microorganisms like fungi and bacteria that live in extremely cold places. All antifreeze proteins bind tightly to ice crystals. However, some crystals form into double-hexagonal pyramids, others into lemon-like shapes. Others, like the antifreeze from snow fleas, have ice crystals shaped like microscopic grains of rice. What other shapes will scientists find in the future?[8]

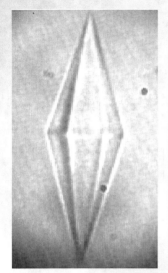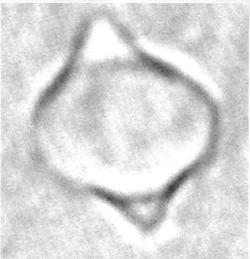

The left crystal was formed by type I AFP and is hexagonal bipyramidal. The lemon-shaped crystal on the right was formed by the hyperactive AFP.

concentration fifty times lower than type I. For this reason, the scientists called the mystery molecule, "hyperactive antifreeze protein."[9]

Marshall, Fletcher, and Davies had discovered how the winter flounder can survive in icy waters. When winter gets really tough and the sea begins to freeze, hyperactive antifreeze proteins in the winter flounder form tiny ice crystals into lemon-like shapes. This protects the flounder from freezing because lemon-shaped crystals do not grow into bigger, deadly, icy masses.

Cod, on the other hand, do not have hyperactive antifreeze proteins. When seawater freezes, nothing prevents large icy masses from growing inside the fish. A necropsy (an examination of a dead animal) revealed that a cod in Hew's tank had died because it had ice in the heart.[10]

Playing With the Freezing Point

Winter flounder, like some other fish, insects, plants, and microorganisms, are able to survive and even thrive in extremely cold environments thanks in part to antifreeze molecules. However, you do not need specialized antifreeze molecules to decrease the freezing point of water. In the following experiments you will learn how to change the freezing point of water in simple ways.

Materials
- ★ table sugar
- ★ table salt
- ★ one 10-oz Styrofoam cup
- ★ test tubes
- ★ thermometer
- ★ measuring cups and measuring spoons
- ★ ice cubes or crushed ice

Procedure
1. Prepare the ice bath:
2. Fill the Styrofoam cup with ice
3. Cover the ice with a layer of salt about a 1/2 inch thick
4. Stir the ice-salt mixture
5. Check that the temperature drops to at least -10°C (14°F)

Experiment
Prepare a salt solution by mixing 5.8 grams (about 1 teaspoon) of salt to 100 milliliters of water (measure 1/2 cup and remove

2 tablespoons of water). Mix well until crystals dissolve. Label this solution "High-salt." Prepare a second salt solution mixing a pinch of salt with 100 milliliters of water. Mix well until crystals dissolve. Label this solution "Low-salt."

Prepare a solution of sugar by mixing 34 grams (1/8 cup) of sugar to 100 milliliters of water. Mix well until crystals dissolve. Label this solution "High-sugar." Prepare a second sugar solution, mixing 3 grams (1/4 teaspoon) of sugar with 100 milliliters of water. Mix well until crystals dissolve. Label this solution "Low-sugar."

Fill a test tube half full with plain water and place it in the ice bath. Stir the water gently with the thermometer as you measure the temperature of the water. Keep an eye on the test tube and record the temperature when the first ice crystals appear on the inside wall of the test tube. This would be the freezing point of plain or pure water. Repeat steps 3 through 5 using the "High" and "Low" solutions you prepared with salt and sugar.

Observe and Answer

What effect does the amount of salt in a solution have on the freezing point of water?

What effect does the amount of sugar in a solution have on the freezing point of water?

Which would freeze quicker in your freezer, a popsicle made with plain water or one made with orange juice?

3
BUBBLEHEADS NEVER HEARD SO WELL

The blind, old catfish living in the aquarium looked like the perfect candidate for the experiment. Karl von Frisch decided that this common fish would help him settle an old scientific dispute once and for all. Can fish hear?

In the 1920s, most scientists thought that fish were deaf. Others had their doubts. Von Frisch thought that one reason scientists were still arguing about it was that the right experiment had not been done. He was going to answer the question with his old catfish.[1]

Training *Ameiurus*

The little catfish, whose scientific name is *Ameiurus nebulosus*, spent most of the day inside a clay pipe at the bottom of the aquarium. Every day, von Frisch dropped food near the opening of the pipe. The catfish perceived the food with its chemical senses (similar to smell), came out of the pipe, and swallowed the food.

To test if the catfish could hear, von Frisch whistled every time, right before he dropped food in the tank. He was training the catfish. He was trying to teach the catfish that the whistle announced that food was coming.

After a few days of whistling and feeding, the catfish came out of its pipe when von Frisch whistled and before he provided the food. The catfish even swam to the surface of the water looking for the food. Because this catfish was blind, von Frisch knew that it could not see him bring the food. Sound had been linked to food in the catfish's mind. It was

THE SPEED OF SOUND

The speed of sound is not always the same. For example, sound travels through air at 343 meters (1,125 feet) per second, but it travels faster through water, 1,493 meters (4,899 feet) per second. Sound travels even faster through solids. Sounds travels through a diamond at 12,000 meters (39,372 feet) per second, and it goes through iron at 5,130 meters (16,832 feet) per second. The speed of sound also depends on the temperature. For example, the warmer the air is, the faster the sound will usually travel through it.[2]

crystal clear that for this to happen, the catfish had to be able to hear the whistle.[3]

The little, old, and blind catfish had finally settled the question: fish do have a sense of hearing. Now scientists were intrigued by another question: how do fish hear sound underwater?

Stones in Their Ears

Von Frisch also studied other types of fish and found that all can hear. Some have better hearing than others. For example, minnows hear better than trout and eels. Each type of fish has pitches they hear best.[4]

Knowing that fish can hear sounds underwater, scientists began to look for the fish's organ for hearing. Fish do not have external ears like people and most other animals do. Scientists looked for internal ears in fish heads. They found

Close up of an elephantnose fish. The electric organ is the narrow reddish area on the tail.

them inside the skull, on either side of the brain and just behind the eyes. They called them "inner ears."

Each inner ear is formed by three sacs. Each sac contains a small "stone," a rounded mineral structure made of calcium carbonate. These are otoliths, or ear stones. Each otolith rests on a jelly-like surface that contains hairy nerve endings. These nerves link the inner ears with the fish's brain.[5]

> **Science Tongue Twister:**
> *The elephantnose fish's scientific name is* **Gnathonemus petersii.**

When sound travels through water, the vibrations continue through the fish's body. When sound reaches the inner ears, it rattles the otoliths, which in turn bend the hairy endings of the nerves. The bending of the nerve endings triggers a signal through the nerves to the brain and the fish perceives the sound.[6]

Bubbles in Their Heads

Von Frisch studied the inner ears of the elephantnose fish. This is an African fish that lives in murky rivers. Von Frisch was intrigued by this fish's ear—a gas bladder, like a bubble, connects directly to one of the three sacs that form the inner ear.[7]

What was the purpose of the bubbles in elephantnose fish ears? Von Frisch did not answer this question. Eighty years after him, American scientists independently uncovered the secret of the bubbles.

Training *Gnathonemus*: Beep and Discharge

John Crawford and Lindsay Fletcher at the University of Pennsylvania used a training method similar to the one von Frisch had used with the catfish.

Von Frisch had trained the catfish to come out of its shelter to eat after hearing a whistle. Elephantnose fish have a specialized organ located along their tails that produces an electric discharge. Crawford and his team trained the fish to produce an electric discharge when it heard a sound. If the fish did not hear a sound, it did not produce a discharge.[8]

> **Meet the Scientists:**
> *John Crawford and Lindsay Fletcher are biologists interested in understanding how fish hear underwater. They performed the experiments with the elephantnose fish at the University of Pennsylvania.*

The scientists then tested whether ear bubbles were important for hearing. Would the elephantnose fish produce a discharge after the air was removed from the bubbles? To remove the air from the bubbles, the scientists flushed it with a saline solution (lightly salted water).[9]

After testing many elephantnose fish with and without air in their bubbles, the scientists uncovered the old secret of the ear bubbles.

Can Fish Hear Me Now?

Elephantnose fish with their ear bubbles intact had very sensitive hearing. But after the air had been displaced from

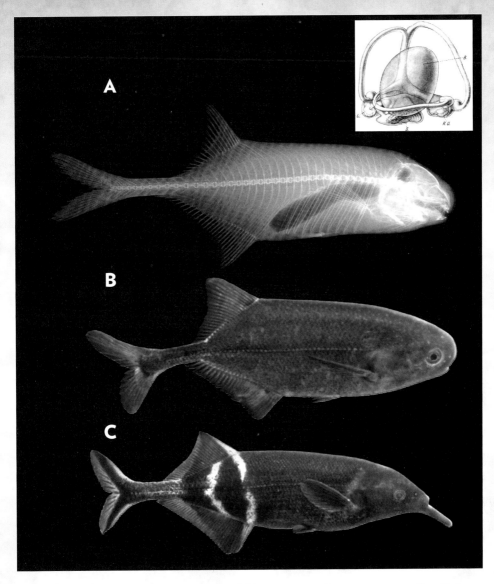

Elephantnose fish at the bottom (C) compared to a very similar fish called *Pollimyrus adspersus*. Both fish are of about the same size (10 cm) and the ear and the swim bladders have similar locations in both fish. The top image (A) is an X-ray of *P. adspersus*. The dark elongated shadow is the swim bladder. The ear bladder shows as a dark spot in the head. The inset at the top is a drawing showing the ear bladder sitting on one of the ear stones. (B: *P. adspersus*)

The elephantnose fish is one of many members of a family of fish called *Mormyridae*. Some of these fish produce sounds like grunts, croaks, hums, moans, thumps, pops, buzzes, clicks, howls, knocks, and snores. Some of the sounds are produced in particular situations, like when looking for a mate or facing a rival. This means that fish can use sound to communicate with others of their kind just as birds and other animals do. But what are they saying? Scientists are trying to find out.[10]

the bubbles, the fish could not hear as well. The fish could still hear sounds of the same pitch, but the sounds had to be 1.6 times louder.[11]

The scientists had proved that the bubbles attached to the inner ear of elephantnose fish increase the fish's sensitivity to sound. The bubbles work like a hearing aid. They allow the fish to perceive faint sounds they would not be able to sense without the bubbles.

With the bubbles intact, elephantnose fish can hear the sounds made by other fish eating. They can also hear the sound of rain falling on the surface of the water and the sounds of predators suddenly lunging toward them.[12] The bubbles help these fish to stay alert and survive in their murky surroundings.

4
FISH GET HOOKED ON DECORATING

Sara Östlund-Nilsson and Mikael Holmlund were observing three-spined stickleback fish build their nests on Sweden's west coast. It has been known for many years that some fish build nests just like birds do. What was intriguing was that the five-centimeter-long (two inches) three-spined sticklebacks added brightly colored red algae to their green algae nests.[1]

Animals usually try to camouflage, or hide, their nests so predators cannot find them. Why were these fish making their nests stand out by adding contrasting bright colors to them?

> **Meet the Scientists:**
> **Sara Östlund-Nilsson and Mikael Holmlund are biologists at the University of Oslo, Norway. They are interested in various aspects of fish reproduction, including paternal care and mate choice.**

Underwater Nest-Building Master

Every spring, when the time comes to find a mate, the cheeks and throats of the three-spined stickleback males turn bright red and their eyes bright blue. Besides changing their colors, the males begin building nests.

First, he digs a pit in the sandy sea bottom. Then, he lays down a mat of long, stringy, usually green algae. The stickleback then covers part of the nest with sand it carries in its mouth. Finally, it forms a tunnel in the nest through which the female will pass during spawning—the process of releasing eggs.

The nest structure is held in place with a "glue" produced in the fish's kidneys. The glue is called "spiggin," after the Swedish name of the fish, "spigg." The fish releases the glue through its cloaca, or rear end. The male takes a few days to glue the ends of the string-like algae together and make the nest structure stronger.[2]

A Single Dad

After they build nests, male sticklebacks compete with each other trying to attract females to spawn in their nests. They spend about ten days collecting eggs and then they stop being interested in females. They concentrate on caring for the eggs. They stay alert for predators and keep them away from the eggs. They make sure the eggs receive enough oxygen to develop into little sticklebacks by fanning oxygen-rich water through the nest. They also remove dead or diseased eggs from the nest.[3]

Male sticklebacks work hard to provide their next generation with a safe place to grow. Why, then, do males add red materials that may give the nest away to predators?

Pick and Choose

Östlund-Nilsson and Holmlund studied the fish in their lab. When the males had developed the red-colored cheeks and throats, the scientists knew that the fish were ready to build nests. Then, the scientists provided the fish with two separate piles of algae, one green and one red. After two days, the

Male three-spined stickleback, showing its red belly and blue eyes, guides a female toward the nest entrance.

Dr. Sara Östlund-Nilsson in her lab.

scientists checked which colors the fish had used to build their nests.

All the males made a nest of the same color algae (most fish made it all green), and marked the nest entrance with algae of a different color. All green algae nests had the entrance marked with red algae strings.[4] Other male animals sometimes display bright colors on their bodies to attract a female. What if male sticklebacks decorated their nests with bright colors to attract females?

Hooked on Decorating

Östlund-Nilsson and Holmlund tested the idea that nest decorating is the male sticklebacks' strategy to lure females to their nests. The scientists provided males with plenty of varied decorations. Given the chance, would male sticklebacks further enhance their nests' decorations?

The scientists provided sticklebacks with ten metal foil sticks and ten spangles in each of the following colors: red, blue, green, yellow, and silver. They also had green algae to build the nests.[5] Would the fish have a color and shape preference? The scientists waited three days to find out.

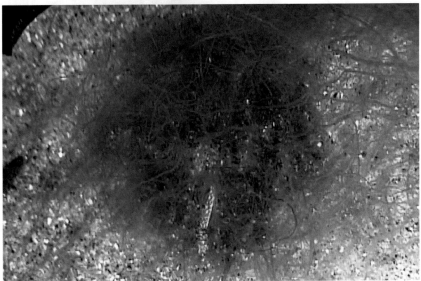

Top view of three-spined stickleback nests in an aquarium showing the green algae and the colorful decorations marking the nest entrance.

All seventeen males tested preferred sticks to spangles to mark the nest entrance. Furthermore, the males preferred red sticks to all the other colored sticks.[6] The scientists now wondered, how will female sticklebacks respond to these colorful displays in the nests?

Sticklebacks Like it Flashy

Östlund-Nilsson and Holmlund tested the reaction of female sticklebacks to flashily decorated nests. They compared it to the reaction to plain, one-color algae nests.

The scientists placed a female in an aquarium that contained males with flashy nests and males with plain nests. All the females tested spent more time—about 86 percent of the time they were in the tank—with the males with flashy decorated nests. The females clearly preferred more artistic sticklebacks to the ones that had no artistic inclinations.[7]

Östlund-Nilsson and Holmlund had uncovered the secret of the artistic male three-spined stickleback. Male sticklebacks decorate their nests with bright, contrasting colors to make them more appealing to spawning females.

5
EYES ON THE STARS

t first glance, this brittle star looked like any other. It had five thin, long, and prickly arms connected to a small disk-shaped body. But when light shone over it, the unusual brittle star did something others did not. It changed color dramatically from uniform brown during the day to banded gray and black at night.

Intrigued, Gordon Hendler continued to observe. He learned that this relative of the sea urchin not only responded to light by changing colors. If a light shone on an outstretched arm, the star would hide as fast as it could. In the wild, this coral-reef dweller can detect shadows and quickly escape from predators into dark holes.[1]

Science Tongue Twister:
The scientific name of the brittle star the scientists studied is **Ophiocoma wendtii.**

35

A PUZZLING CREATURE

The brittle star scientists studied here is one of the most common animals in the Caribbean reefs. Even so, it was very hard for Hendler and other scientists to understand it at the beginning. At first, Hendler thought that this brittle star was not one species but two, which were identical in shape, but not in color. One type was brown and the other was banded in gray and black. After a few experiments, Hendler realized that there were not two species but only one that could change colors from day to night and back again![2]

Hendler was curious. This type of reaction is usually expected in animals with eyes. Brittle stars are sensitive to light, but they do not have organs that look like eyes. How do they see? Hendler and his colleagues placed brittle stars under the microscope to find out.

A Glassy Exoskeleton

The brittle star is an echinoderm. Echinoderms have two unique characteristics that distinguish them from other animals. First, their bodies are divided into five equal parts. That is easy to see in brittle stars with their five arms. The second unique characteristic is that echinoderms have a series of canals on the outside of their bodies. Water runs through

Brittle stars change color depending on the amount of light in their environment. Here is the same brittle star showing lighter colors and gray bands at night and deep brown coloration in the daytime.

the canals transporting food, other nutrients, and gases. Echinoderms play a very important role in their environment. Some of them feed on the waste of other animals. They work as garbage collectors and help keep their environment healthy.[3]

Brittle stars are boneless creatures with bodies supported by a hard skeleton on the outside. This is the exoskeleton. Brittle stars' exoskeletons are made of calcite or calcium carbonate, which is the same as chalk.

When scientists inspected brittle stars under the microscope, they saw that the exoskeletons were hard and opaque on the bottom. But on the top, the stars were covered with numerous spherical (or dome-like) hard, transparent structures also made of calcium carbonate.[4]

The scientists compared light-sensitive brittle stars with brittle stars that do not react to light. They discovered that only the light-sensitive species have special tiny, round, transparent structures on their skeletons. These structures look like a sphere cut in half—just like tiny hard contact lenses. But, do they work like lenses?

A New Type of Eye

If you inspect a brittle star closely, you will not find structures that resemble eyes as we know them. However, the stars are not completely blind in the reef. They definitely use visual clues to move around safely and to find food and shelter.

Scientists wondered, does an eye have to look like an eye to be an eye? What if nature has developed ways we had not imagined to use calcite to make lens-type structures?

Focus on the Stars

To find out if the clear, dome-like structures on the top of brittle stars worked like lenses, Hendler partnered with Joanna Aizenberg and her colleagues at Bell Laboratories and the Weizman Institute of Science. Aizenberg is an expert in optical structures, or structures that interact with light, like lenses.

Aizenberg reasoned that if the dome-like structures worked like lenses, then they should be able to focus light on a specific point under them, like lenses do. Think of using a magnifying glass to focus sunlight on a piece of paper to burn it.[6] In a similar way, the scientists used the tiny, clear, dome-like structures of brittle stars to try to focus light on a special film and leave a mark.

Meet the Scientists:
Gordon Hendler and his colleagues are biologists at the Natural History Museum in Los Angeles. They study echinoderms, which include sea stars, brittle stars, sea urchins, sea cucumbers, and feather stars. Echinoderms live in marine waters all over the world.[5]

Joanna Aizenberg and her colleagues work at Bell Laboratories in New Jersey and at the Weizman Institute of Science in Israel. They are experts in optics; they study light and vision through lenses and other optical structures. They are interested in how living creatures create and use optical structures for their survival.

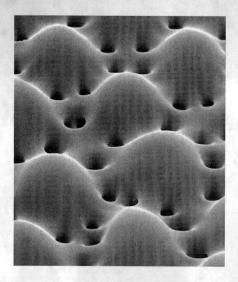

Magnified view of the array of microlenses in the brittle star.

This is called a lithographic experiment.[7]

The scientists placed a group of clear brittle star domes over the special film and shone light through the lenses. When they looked at the film they saw that the light had burned dots on the film. The dots were arranged in the same pattern as the domes they had placed above the film, one dot beneath each dome.[8]

This meant that each clear dome had focused a tiny ray of light. The scientists were thrilled! They had proof that the thousands of transparent domes on brittle stars worked like lenses. But could the brittle star sense the light?

The Nerve Connection

The scientists had made another discovery that suggested that the domes might work like eyes for the brittle star. They saw nerve bundles under the clear, lens-like structures. The nerves were located right at the focus point of the domes. Furthermore, these nerves fired a signal when light entered through the domes.[9] This meant that the nerves transmitted information through the animal's nervous system when light went through the domes. But what does it see?

Pixel by Pixel

Aizenberg, Hendler, and their colleagues think that brittle stars' eyes may work like a compound eye. In this type of eye, each lens provides one tiny section of the whole image. Like a puzzle in which each piece provides a small part of the whole image, each lens in the brittle star provides one piece of

WEARING "SHADES"

The color changes displayed by light-sensitive brittle stars occur when pigment-containing cells move to or from the surface of the star. The star gets its dark color during the day because the pigment cells move to the surface of the star. It looks like the color of the pigment, or dark brown. The opposite occurs at night. The pigment cells move away from the surface of the star. It then looks lighter in color.

The pigment cells also work like sunglasses for the brittle stars. When the pigment cells move to the surface, they cover the lenses with their dark color. This reduces the intensity of the light on the lenses, just like when you wear shades.[10]

Bell Labs researchers Alexei Tkachenko and Joanna Aizenberg were involved in the study of brittle stars.

what the brittle star sees. Like a digital camera that builds an image pixel by pixel, the tiny lenses on a brittle star create an image lens by lens.[11]

The secret has been solved. Brittle stars do not have eyes like people, but if you go diving in a coral reef and see a shy brittle star, it might be watching you!

★ CHAPTER NOTES ★

Chapter 1. Slick and Slime

1. Interview with Dr. Douglas Fudge, May 15, 2007.
2. Interview with Dr. Douglas Fudge, October 19, 2004.
3. Douglas Fudge, et al., "Composition, Morphology, and Mechanics of Hagfish Slime," *Journal of Experimental Biology*, vol. 208, 2005, pp. 4613–4614, 4617.
4. Interview with Dr. Douglas Fudge, May 15, 2007.
5. Fudge, et al., p. 4620.
6. Jeanette Lim, et al., "Hagfish Slime Ecomechanics: Testing the Gill-clogging Hypothesis," *Journal of Experimental Biology*, vol. 209, 2006, pp. 703–704.
7. Jørgen Mørup Jørgensen, ed., *Biology of Hagfishes* (London: Chapman and Hall, 1998), p. 302.
8. Lim, et al., p. 706.
9. Ibid.

Chapter 2. Fish Fight the Big Freeze

1. Choy Hew, "Stories Behind Discovery. Serendipity & Perseverance: The Career of a Marine Biologist," University of Singapore, n.d., <http://www.dbs.nus.edu.sg/hcl/stories_behind _discovery.html> (October 2, 2007).
2. Ibid.
3. Interview with Dr. Christopher Marshall, May 25, 2007.
4. Ibid.
5. Christopher B. Marshall, Garth L. Fletcher, and Peter L. Davies, "Hyperactive Antifreeze Proteins in a Fish," *Nature*, vol. 429, no. 6988, 2004, p. 153.
6. Ibid.
7. Michael J. Kuiper, et al., "Purification of Antifreeze Proteins by Adsorption to Ice," *Biochemical and Biophysical Research*

Communications, vol. 300, no. 3, 2003, p. 646.

8. Laurie A. Graham, et al., "Glycine-rich Antifreeze Proteins From Snow Fleas," *Science*, vol. 310, no. 5747, October 21, 2005, p. 461.

9. Marshall, Fletcher, and Davies, p. 153.

10. Hew.

Chapter 3. Bubbleheads Never Heard So Well

1. Karl von Frisch, "The Sense of Hearing in Fish," *Nature*, vol. 141, 1938, p. 8.

2. "Speed of Sound in Various Bulk Media," Georgia State University, n.d., <http://hyperphysics.phy-astr.gsu.edu/hbase/tables/soundv.html> (October 2, 2007).

3. von Frisch, p. 8.

4. Ibid.

5. Stephan Reebs, *Fish Behavior in the Aquarium and in the Wild* (Ithaca, N.Y.: Cornell University Press, 2001), p. 27.

6. Ibid.

7. von Frisch, p. 11.

8. Lindsay Fletcher and John Crawford, "Acoustic Detection by Sound-producing Fishes (Mormyridae): The Role of Gas-filled Tympanic Bladders," *The Journal of Experimental Biology*, vol. 204, no. 2, 2001, p. 175.

9. Ibid., p. 178.

10. Ibid., p. 181.

11. Ibid., p. 179.

12. Ibid., p. 181.

Chapter 4. Fish Get Hooked on Decorating

1. Sara Östlund-Nilsson and Mikael Holmlund, "The Artistic Three-spined Stickleback (*Gasterosteus aculeatus*)," *Behavioral Ecology and Sociobiology*, vol. 53, no. 4, March 2003, pp. 214, 217.

2. Sara Östlund-Nilsson, et al., eds., *The Biology of the Three-*

spined Stickleback (Boca Raton, Fla.: CRC Press Marine Science Series, 2007), p. 121.

3. Ibid, p. 139.
4. Östlund-Nilsson and Holmlund, p. 217.
5. Ibid.
6. Interview with Dr. Sara Östlund-Nilsson, June 28, 2007.
7. Ibid.

Chapter 5. Eyes on the Stars

1. Interview with Dr. Gordon Hendler, May 31, 2007.
2. Ibid.
3. David Krogh, *Biology: A Guide to the Natural World*, 3rd ed. (Upper Saddle River, N.J.: Pearson Prentice Hall, 2005), p. 465.
4. Gordon Hendler and Maria Byrne, "Fine Structure of the Dorsal Arm Plate of *Ophiocoma wendtii*: Evidence for a Photoreceptor System (Echinodermata, Ophiuroidea)," *Zoomorphology*, vol. 107, 1987, pp. 262–264.
5. Gordon Hendler, et al., *Sea Stars, Sea Urchins, and Allies* (Washington, D.C.: Smithsonian Institution Press, 1995), p. 112.
6. Interview with Dr. Joanna Aizenberg, December 12, 2001.
7. Joanna Aizenberg, et al., "Calcitic Microlenses as Part of the Photoreceptor System in Brittlestars," *Nature*, vol. 412, August 23, 2001, pp. 819, 820.
8. Ibid., p. 820.
9. Jim Cobb and Gordon Hendler, "Neurophysiological Characterization of the Photoreceptor System in a Brittlestar, *Ophiocoma wendtii* (Echinodermata: Ophiuroidea)," *Comparative Biochemistry and Physiology*, vol. 97A, no. 3, 1990, p. 330.
10. Hendler and Byrne, p. 264.
11. Aizenberg, et al., p. 821.

★ GLOSSARY ★

antifreeze ★ A substance that prevents liquids from freezing.

calcite ★ Colorless or white mineral made of calcium carbonate and used to make glass, cement, chalk, and paint.

camouflage ★ To hide by imitating the colors of the environment.

carrion ★ Rotting animal flesh.

denature ★ To modify a molecule's structure by chemical or physical means.

exoskeleton ★ The hard covering on the outside of organisms.

gill ★ The breathing organ of a fish.

lens ★ A transparent piece of glass for focusing.

mucin ★ A complex protein present in mucus.

necropsy ★ A medical examination of a dead animal.

nerve ★ A bundle of fibers that transmits messages through the nervous system.

offspring ★ An animal's young.

optics ★ The study of light.

otoliths ★ Small grains of calcium carbonate in the inner ear of some animals.

pigment ★ A substance that is added to give something, like paint, its color.

pincer ★ A tool for gripping things.

predator ★ An animal that hunts, kills, and eats other animals to survive.

spawn ★ To produce and deposit eggs.

viscous ★ Thick and sticky.

★ FURTHER READING ★

Books

Dawes, John. *Fish: Spiny-finned Fish 1, Vol. 40: Sticklebacks, Sea Horses, Gurnards, Flounder*. Danbury, Conn.: Grolier, 2005.

Gilpin, Daniel. *Starfish, Urchins, and Other Echinoderms*. Minneapolis, Minn.: Compass Point Books, 2006.

McCourt, Lisa and Cheryl Nathan. *Wet 'n' Weird: The Strangest Sea Creatures You Ever Saw*. Los Angeles: Lowell House Juvenile, 2001.

Reebs, Stephan. *Fish Behavior in the Aquarium and in the Wild*. Ithaca, N.Y.: Cornell University Press, 2001.

Internet Addresses

Natural History Museum of Los Angeles County, Current Online Exhibits
http://www.nhm.org/exhibitions/online.html

Hear the Electric Discharges of the Elephantnose Fish
http://sci-toys.com/scitoys/scitoys/biology/electric_fish/electric_fish.htm

Ana María Rodríguez's Homepage
http://www.anamariarodriguez.com/

★ INDEX ★